USING SCIENCE
BE A SHARK
BIOLOGIST

By Suzy Gazlay

Shark Consultant: Salvador Jorgensen

Series Consultant: Kirk A. Janowiak

USING
SCIENCE
BE A SHARK
BIOLOGIST

by Suzy Gazlay
Shark Consultant: Salvador Jorgensen
Series Consultant: Kirk A. Janowiak
ticktock project editor: Jo Hanks
ticktock designer: Graham Rich
With thanks to: Sara Greasley and Anna Brett

Copyright © ticktock Entertainment Ltd 2008
First published in Great Britain in 2008 by ticktock Media Ltd.,
Unit 2, Orchard Business Centre, North Farm Road, Tunbridge Wells, Kent, TN2 3XF

ISBN 978 1 84696 619 4 pbk
ISBN 978 1 84696 681 1 hbk
Printed in China
9 8 7 6 5 4 3 2

SUZY GAZLAY

Suzy Gazlay (MA Integrated Math/Science Education) is a teacher and writer who has worked with students of all ages. She has also served as a science specialist, curriculum developer, and consultant in varying capacities. She is the recipient of a Presidential Award for Excellence in Math and Science Teaching. Now retired from fulltime classroom teaching, she continues to write, consult, and work with educators and children, particularly in science and music education. Her many interests include music, environmental issues, marine biology, and the outdoors.

KIRK A. JANOWIAK

BS Biology & Natural Resources, MS Ecology & Animal Behaviour, MS Science Education. Kirk has enjoyed teaching students from preschool through to college age. He has been awarded the National Association of Biology Teachers' Outstanding Biology Teacher Award and was honoured to be a finalist for the Presidential Award for Math and Science Teaching. Kirk currently teaches Biology and Environmental Science and enjoys a wide range of interests from music to the art of roasting coffee.

SALVADOR JORGENSEN PhD

Salvador is a postdoctoral scholar working at Stanford University's Hopkins Marine Station and the Monterey Bay Aquarium in California, USA. He is researching the movement and population structure of white sharks in the eastern Pacific Ocean using tagging and genetics. During graduate school Dr Jorgensen performed his field studies as a Fulbright scholar in Mexico's Gulf of California (Sea of Cortez), studying the movements of tuna and scalloped hammerhead sharks around seamounts.

CONTENTS

This book supports the teaching of science at Key Stage 2 of the National Curriculum. Students will develop their understanding of these areas of scientific inquiry:

- Ideas and evidence in science
- Investigative skills
- Obtaining and presenting evidence
- Considering and evaluating evidence

Students will also learn about:

- Varieties of sharks
- Shark physiology
- How sharks breathe
- Shark necropsies and causes of death
- Hydrodynamics and underwater propulsion
- Shark behaviour
- Food chains and webs
- Cold-blooded and warm-bodied fish
- What sharks eat
- Why shark attacks happen
- Tagging and tracking sharks
- Keeping sharks in captivity
- Keeping safe around sharks
- Shark populations and conservation

HOW TO USE THIS BOOK

Science is important in the lives of people everywhere. We use science at home and at school – in fact, all the time. Everybody needs to know about science to understand how the world works. A shark biologist needs to understand science in order to gather information about shark behaviour. A biologist uses this information to educate people and protect sharks. With this book, you'll use science to track and research them.

This exciting science book is very easy to use – check out what's inside!

INTRODUCTION

Fun to read information about being a shark biologist.

FACTFILE

Easy to understand information about how shark biology works.

STAYING WARM IN COLD WATER

The Sun is rising as you and your crew head out to sea. Your destination is an elephant seal colony on a remote beach up the coast. Great white sharks will be waiting offshore, waiting for an opportunity to catch their next meal. Elephant seals aren't easy prey. These massive beasts have lots of blubber. They can weigh more than 2,200 kilograms! If the shark doesn't strike just right, an elephant seal can put up a tough fight. You've seen great white sharks with the scars to prove it!

🦈 FACTFILE

If you were cold-blooded, like most fish, your body temperature would be 4°C.

- Great white sharks are warm-bodied. This means they can swim fast and survive in cold water where seals live.
- Digestion, swimming, and other muscular activities generate heat.
- This heat is lost from the body surface of most fish. In great white sharks, their powerful muscles are near the centre of their body. This is where most of their blood is, away from the skin where heat can be lost.

16

WORKSTATION

Real life conservation experiences, situations and problems for you to read about.

CHALLENGE QUESTIONS

Now that you understand the science, put it into practice.

WORKSTATION

You've been gathering data about the types of prey eaten by great white sharks along this coast.

Great white sharks have to be picky eaters because they need high-fat food for fuel. Seals have lots of blubber, more than most other prey–they are a shark's ideal dinner!

Now, as your boat approaches the seal colony, you see a great white shark attack a young elephant seal. You add it to your list of great white prey (below).

Elephant seal: 25

California sea lion: 15

Dead whale carcass: 6

Northern fur seal: 10

Pelican: 2

Jellyfish: 1

Sea turtle: 3

Seagull: 1

Other sharks: 5

Tuna: 6

Halibut: 4

Mackerel: 8

Harbor seal: 15

Salmon: 6

Porpoise: 1

CHALLENGE QUESTIONS

1. Which four kinds of prey were attacked most often?
2. What do these four animals have in common?
3. Why would seals be a particularly good choice of food?
4. Why would a dead whale be a good choice of food for a great white shark?

IF YOU NEED HELP!

TIPS FOR SCIENCE SUCCESS

On page 30 you will find lots of tips to help you with your science work.

ANSWERS

Turn to page 31 to check your answers. (*Try all the activities and questions before you take a look at the answers.*)

GLOSSARY

On page 32 there is a glossary of shark conservation and science words.

SHARK BIOLOGIST

The sign on your office door says that you are a shark biologist. Your laboratory sits on a large bay that opens into the Pacific Ocean. You study many different things about sharks. Where do they spend their time? How far do they travel? Where do they go? You learn about sharks by visiting the places where they gather. As a biologist, you help to protect sharks. Sometimes you are asked to talk to school groups visiting a local aquarium.

FACTFILE

- There are more than 460 known species of sharks.
- Some sharks lay eggs that hatch in the water. In other species, babies are born live and free-swimming.
- Most sharks live in salt water, but some live in fresh water.
- Sharks can be found in shallow and very deep waters.
- Some sharks stick close to home, but others travel long distances.
- Sharks cannot swim backwards. Most must swim forward in order to breathe.
- Sharks do not normally attack people.

A school of grey reef sharks are looking for food.

WORKSTATION

You show your audience photographs of different types of sharks from all over the world. They are amazed by the diversity, or variety of species.

Name	Whale shark	Great white shark	Oceanic whitetip shark
Length	Up to 14 metres	Up to 7 metres	Up to 4 metres
Diet	Plankton, small fish	Fish, marine mammals	Fish, turtles, birds, rubbish

Name	Sawfish shark	Spined pygmy shark	Frilled shark
Length	Up to 7.5 metres	18-20 centimetres	Up to 2 metres
Diet	Fish, shellfish, squid	Squid, shrimp, fish	Squid, fish

Name	Goblin shark	Scalloped hammerhead shark	Wobbegong shark
Length	2-3 metres	Up to 4.5 metres	Up to 3 metres
Diet	Fish, squid, crabs	Fish, rays, squid, shellfish	Fish, shellfish, octopus

CHALLENGE QUESTIONS

You study the chart above to answer the following questions:

1. Which is the largest shark?
2. Which is the smallest?
3. How many grow to three metres or more?
4. Name three foods eaten by most of these sharks.

THE DESIGN OF A SHARK

As a shark expert, you're often asked to provide information for the public. Today you're designing a display for your local aquarium. You want to show the basic structure that is common to all sharks. Sharks can look very different from one another. Even so, they are all built along the same lines.

A **pectoral fin** on each side helps with swimming, balance, and turning.

A pair of **pelvic fins** helps with stability and mating.

 All sharks have a similar skeleton.

- It is made of strong, flexible cartilage.
- It's the same material that gives shape to your ears.
- Its flexibility allows a shark to make tight turns.
- It is lighter than bone and helps keep the shark from sinking.

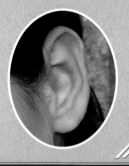

This hammerhead shark has some very strange features! Even so, it has the same structure as other sharks.

orsal
for
eering.

The strong **caudal fin**, or tail, pushes the shark through the water.

The **anal fin** is used for balance and stability.

WORKSTATION

These are some of the interesting physical features of sharks.

SHARK SKIN

- A shark's skin is covered with denticles. This picture shows what denticles look like under a microscope.
- Most denticles point backward. Rubbing the shark from front to back feels smooth. Rubbing the other way can cause injury.
- The shape of the denticles reduces friction with the water. The shark can swim more efficiently and quietly.

SHARK SNOUT

- The shark's nostrils are used for smelling, not breathing.
- A keen sense of smell helps a shark to find food.

SHARK TEETH

- Some sharks have up to 3,000 teeth at any one time.
- The teeth are arranged in rows, usually about 5 rows at a time.
- If a tooth is worn down, damaged, or lost, a tooth in the next row replaces it.

Q CHALLENGE QUESTIONS

Now you need some questions to add to your display.

1. What happens when a shark loses or damages a tooth?
2. Why does a shark's skin feel rough?
3. What are the five different types of fins?
4. Which fins have the most to do with changing direction?

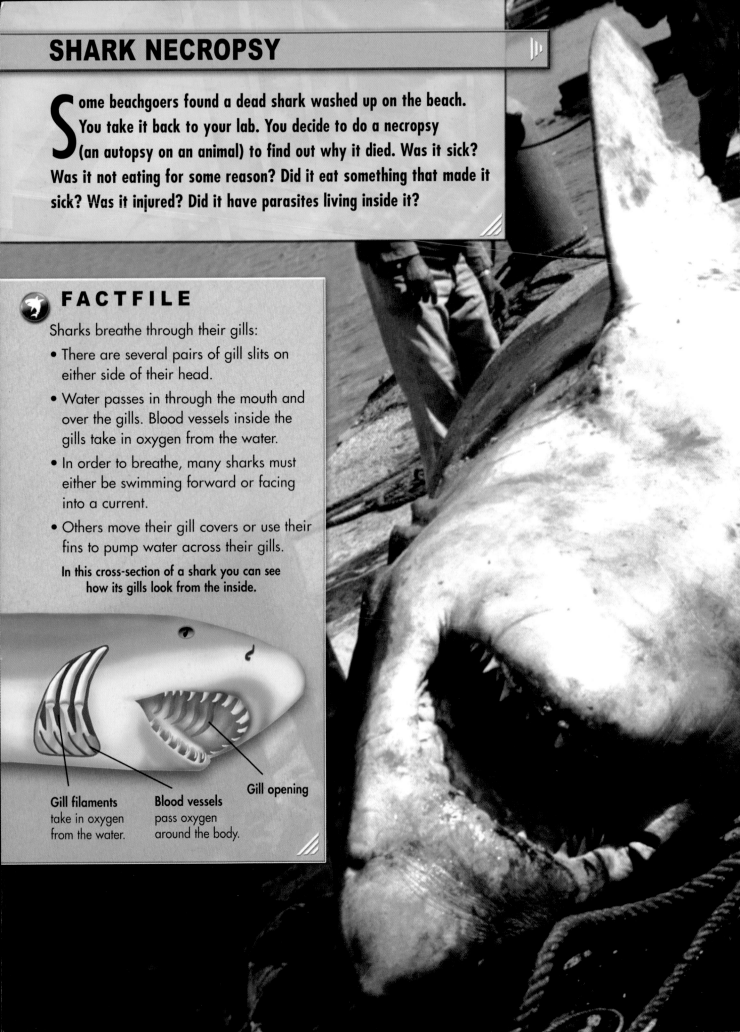

SHARK NECROPSY

Some beachgoers found a dead shark washed up on the beach. You take it back to your lab. You decide to do a necropsy (an autopsy on an animal) to find out why it died. Was it sick? Was it not eating for some reason? Did it eat something that made it sick? Was it injured? Did it have parasites living inside it?

🦈 FACTFILE

Sharks breathe through their gills:

- There are several pairs of gill slits on either side of their head.
- Water passes in through the mouth and over the gills. Blood vessels inside the gills take in oxygen from the water.
- In order to breathe, many sharks must either be swimming forward or facing into a current.
- Others move their gill covers or use their fins to pump water across their gills.

In this cross-section of a shark you can see how its gills look from the inside.

Gill filaments take in oxygen from the water.

Blood vessels pass oxygen around the body.

Gill opening

You put the shark on the lab table and get to work:

First you look for signs of injury:

- You don't see cuts or bruising that might have come from fighting.

- There are no scrapes or bruises that could be the result of being hit by a boat.

You carefully cut into the shark's belly. The first thing you see is the liver. It looks normal.

- The liver stores extra fats as oil.

- The liver helps the shark float because the oil in it is lighter than water.

Next you look at the shark's gills. Under the microscope you see a likely reason why this shark died.

- Its gills are heavily infested with tiny, shrimp-like parasites called copepods.

- They feed on skin and blood.

- They can cause the shark to become weak because it doesn't get enough oxygen.

This is a basking shark with its liver circled. The liver is a shark's largest organ. It can be as much as 25% of the shark's total weight.

A marine copepod.

This great white shark died when it was caught in a fishing net. Its injuries were caused by struggling against the net.

Q CHALLENGE QUESTIONS

You fill out a report listing what you found:

1. What caused the shark to die?

2. The largest organ in the shark's body was not the cause of death. What was that organ?

3. How do you know the shark wasn't attacked by another shark?

4. What four things can a shark do to keep water flowing across its gills?

LEAPING SHARKS!

You've worked with sharks for a long time, but you're still amazed at some of the things they do. This is one of those moments. As you and your team watch in awe, a great white shark suddenly breaks through the surface of the water. All five metres of its magnificent body arches through the air. In a moment it is gone as it dives back into the water, showering you with spray. Why would such a large, heavy animal breach (propel itself out of the water) like that?

 FACTFILE

In spite of its size and weight, the body of a great white shark is actually well-designed to breach.

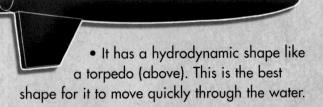

• It has a hydrodynamic shape like a torpedo (above). This is the best shape for it to move quickly through the water.

• The strong ridge at the base of the tail works with the powerful muscles in the mid-body. Together they propel the shark out of the water.

Why does a great white shark breach?
To answer this question, you need to make some observations and look for clues. Then you can make a hypothesis, or reasonable explanation.

- If sharks are breaching while feeding, you'll probably see prey nearby.

- If their breaching has to do with mating behaviour, you'll probably see potential mates nearby.

You can't always see everything! After observing eight different great white sharks breaching, your notes look like this:

Breaching shark	Male or female?	Other sharks observed?	Prey items observed?
A	Male	None	None
B	Female	1 female	1 seal
C	Female	2 males	1 sea lion
D	Male	2 males	1 seal
E	Female	None	1 sea lion
F	Male	None	1 seal, 1 tuna
G	Female	1 female, 1 male	None
H	Male	1 male	1 seal

Q CHALLENGE QUESTIONS

1. How many times was a shark of the opposite sex seen in the area?

2. How many times were seals or sea lions present?

3. Do you think it is more likely that sharks breach because of feeding or mating behaviour?

4. Why did you reach this conclusion?

TOP PREDATORS

As top predators, sharks play an important role in keeping marine life balanced. You've heard that there aren't many hammerhead sharks left in the Sea of Cortez in Mexico. They have been hunted and killed. But they were the top predators! What will happen to the marine life there if they are gone? You decide to investigate.

 FACTFILE

In every habitat, large or small, all living things are part of a food web. Producers make their own food. Consumers get the food they need by eating producers and other consumers. This is a sequence of who eats what.

Secondary carnivores eat other carnivores. They are usually high-level predators, that are not eaten by anything else.

↑

Primary carnivores eat omnivores and herbivores.

↑

1.
Herbivores eat plants.

2.
Omnivores eat both plants and animals.

↑

Producers (such as plants) make their own food.

Sea of Cortez Food Chain Investigation

Both primary and secondary carnivores are predators. If a predator is removed from a food chain, the population of animals that it used to eat will increase. Then there will be more of those animals to eat the animals below them on the food chain.

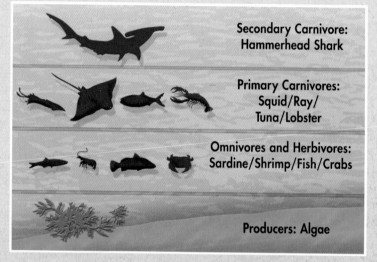

Secondary Carnivore: Hammerhead Shark

Primary Carnivores: Squid/Ray/ Tuna/Lobster

Omnivores and Herbivores: Sardine/Shrimp/Fish/Crabs

Producers: Algae

To find out who eats what, you look inside the stomachs of three of the predators. Here's what you find:

Sardine	Hammerhead shark	Squid
Tiny crabs	Rays	Crabs
Shrimp	Tuna	Shrimp
Algae	Squid	Sardine
Fish eggs	Lobster	Fish

Q CHALLENGE QUESTIONS

1. Put sardines, hammerhead sharks, and squid in order in a food chain, from highest to lowest level.

2. If hammerheads are gone from the Sea of Cortez, which populations of animals will probably increase?

3. If the squid population increases, which animals will be eaten in even greater numbers?

4. What could happen to the sardine population if the sharks are gone? Why?

STAYING WARM IN COLD WATER

The Sun is rising as you and your crew head out to sea. Your destination is an elephant seal colony on a remote beach up the coast. Great white sharks will be waiting offshore, waiting for an opportunity to catch their next meal. Elephant seals aren't easy prey. These massive beasts have lots of blubber. They can weigh more than 2,200 kilograms! If the shark doesn't strike just right, an elephant seal can put up a tough fight. You've seen great white sharks with the scars to prove it!

🦈 FACTFILE

If you were cold-blooded, like most fish, your body temperature would be 4°C.

- Great white sharks are warm-bodied. This means they can swim fast and survive in cold water where seals live.

- Digestion, swimming, and other muscular activities generate heat.

- This heat is lost from the body surface of most fish. In great white sharks, their powerful muscles are near the centre of their body. This is where most of their blood is, away from the skin where heat can be lost.

You've been gathering data about the types of prey eaten by great white sharks along this coast.

Great white sharks have to be picky eaters because they need high-fat food for fuel. They may eat other prey, but animals with lots of blubber are their food of choice. Seals are a shark's ideal dinner!

Now, as your boat approaches the seal colony, you see a great white shark attack a young elephant seal. You add it to your list of great white prey (below).

Elephant seal: 25

California sea lion: 15

Dead whale carcass: 6

Northern fur seal: 10

Pelican: 2

Jellyfish: 1

Sea turtle: 3

Seagull: 1

Other sharks: 5

Tuna: 6

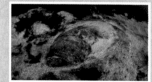

Halibut: 4

Mackerel: 8

Harbour seal: 15

Salmon: 6

Porpoise: 1

Q CHALLENGE QUESTIONS

1. Which four kinds of prey were attacked most often?
2. What do these four animals have in common?
3. Why would seals be a particularly good choice of food?
4. Why would a dead whale be a good choice of food for a great white shark?

HIT OR MISS?

Your phone rings. It's a reporter who wants information about great white sharks. A surfer has been attacked near a beach in southern California. Thankfully, the surfer was not injured – just badly frightened. His surfboard, however, is a different story. The shark took a huge bite of it, leaving jagged teeth marks. The reporter thinks, as many people do, that sharks have poor eyesight. Otherwise, why would this one have bitten the board instead of the surfer? You explain what really happened.

 FACTFILE

You tell the reporter that shark attacks are rare. Furthermore, many more people are injured or die from encounters with other animals. You have the data to back up your statement.

Animal	Approximate number of human deaths in USA from 1990-1999
Deer (collisions with cars)	300
Bears	29
Dogs	18
Snakes	15
Mountain lions	6
Sharks	4
Alligators	2
Wolves	0

The attack on the surfer was a case of mistaken identity.

- Many sharks actually have very good eyesight.
- When a shark sees something that might be food, it tests it by taking a bite. If it doesn't like what it tastes, it spits out the mouthful and swims away.

This great white shark is taste-testing an underwater camera.

You explain to the reporter about how a great white shark attacks its prey.

- It swims below the surface, looking upwards.
- When it sees potential prey, it stalks it from below.
- When the shark attacks prey at the surface, it swims nearly straight up at lightning-fast speed.
- If the target is small, such as a fish or seal, the shark gulps it down whole.

Human Surfer   Sea Turtle   Sea Lion

You can see by looking at these pictures how a shark could mistake a surfer for another animal.

- If the prey is larger, such as a sea lion, the shark takes a huge bite. It then retreats and waits for the prey to bleed to death. Then the shark returns to eat it.

Q CHALLENGE QUESTIONS

1. According to your chart, which two animals were responsible for fewer deaths than sharks?

2. Why would a shark mistake a human surfer for a seal?

3. The shark in the picture above didn't eat the camera after all. Why not?

TAGGING SHARKS

There are many things you want to find out about sharks' behaviour. Are there times when they stay close to one area? How far can they travel in a day? Do they stay in groups? Do they swim about in search of food, or do they follow a predictable pattern of migration? To answer these questions, you need to track individual sharks. You can do this by tagging them, in two different ways.

FACTFILE

Electronic satellite tags follow long distance migration.

- They record data such as when a shark dives, for how long, and how deep.
- They relay one geographic position a day. The data shows how far the shark travelled and where it ended up.
- The data is broadcast by satellite.
- The tag is programmed to break loose at a certain time and pop up to the ocean's surface.
- It sends out a signal so it can be retrieved and its data analysed.

Acoustic tags are used to track short distance travel.

- Receivers are placed underwater at certain sites.
- Tags give off high frequency clicks.
- Receivers pick up the signals as tagged sharks swim past.
- They show if a shark is hanging around or revisiting the area.
- They tell how many times the shark was there and when it arrived.

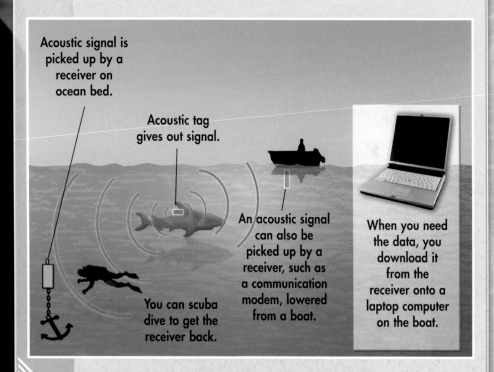

Acoustic signal is picked up by a receiver on ocean bed.

Acoustic tag gives out signal.

You can scuba dive to get the receiver back.

An acoustic signal can also be picked up by a receiver, such as a communication modem, lowered from a boat.

When you need the data, you download it from the receiver onto a laptop computer on the boat.

Q CHALLENGE QUESTIONS

Which type of tag would you use for each of these situations?

1. A shark has been visiting two different feeding grounds about 40 kilometres apart. You want to know how often it goes to each place.

2. Every October and November, several sharks show up around an island. You don't see them again until the following year. You want to find out where they have been.

3. You see sharks near the seal colony during the day. You want to know if they are there at night. It's too dangerous to take a boat out there at night.

4. You've tracked two sharks all the way to Hawaii, USA, and back. You want to know if they will return next year, following the same route.

21

Back at the lab, you check on the whereabouts of some of the sharks you tagged a year ago. You've been using acoustic tags to keep track of the feeding grounds they've been visiting. You're looking at two locations in particular. One is a seal colony on an isolated point of land along the coast. The other is another seal colony on an island about 32 kilometres offshore. You want to know if the sharks stick to one location or if they travel back and forth.

🦈 FACTFILE

This map shows the route a great white shark swam in 2004. It is thought to be the first time scientists were able to confirm that sharks make intercontinental journeys. The data about the shark's journey was gathered using an electronic satellite tag. You also used photographic identification of the shark's unique fin.

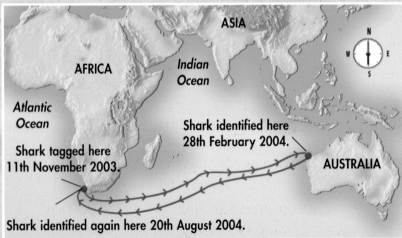

ASIA

AFRICA

Indian
Ocean

N
W   E
S

Atlantic
Ocean

Shark identified here
28th February 2004.

Shark tagged here
11th November 2003.

AUSTRALIA

Shark identified again here 20th August 2004.

WORKSTATION

Your data shows the year-long tracking of five different sharks at two seal colonies.

Each shark is represented by a different colour. Every week a shark is detected at one of the colonies, a dot of its colour appears on the graph.

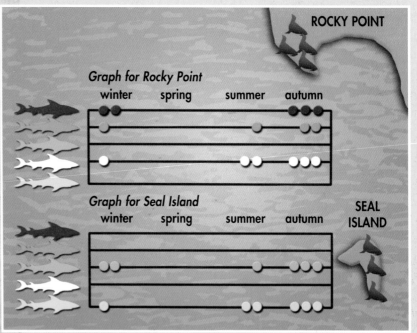

ROCKY POINT

Graph for Rocky Point
winter   spring   summer   autumn

Graph for Seal Island
winter   spring   summer   autumn

SEAL ISLAND

You can use the tags to find out:

- When the sharks visited either or both sites.
- The depth and temperature of the location.

As you look at the data, you can see whether the sharks:

- Show territorial behaviour (where one shark tries to keep the site for itself).
- Visit both sites or just one of them.
- Move to certain places in certain seasons.
- Have a certain pattern to their behaviour.

Q CHALLENGE QUESTIONS

1. During how many weeks did the blue shark show up at the island during the summer? During the winter?
2. During which season are there more visits to both locations?
3. Are the sharks present at either location all year long?
4. Do any of them move back and forth between the two colonies?

TAGGING THE HAMMERHEADS

You're on an exciting adventure that has taken you to the Sea of Cortez in Mexico. Your mission is to tag hammerhead sharks that gather around a seamount (submerged mountain) there. You know that they leave the seamount every evening at sundown. You want to find out how far they travel and where they go. This time, however, you won't be tagging them from a boat. You'll be diving among the hammerheads as you tag them.

 ## FACTFILE

You've observed some interesting things about hammerheads.

- There can be hundreds of them in a single school.
- They feed on fish, octopus, squid, and crustaceans such as crabs.
- Their cruising speed is about three kilometres per hour.

This particular type of hammerhead shark has never been known to attack a human. Still, they're sharks, so you're careful as you dive among them.

- You'll be using both types of tags (electronic and acoustic).
- You can tag the hammerheads by free-diving or scuba diving.
- Satellite tags track long-term movements and diving behaviour.
- The acoustic tag data will allow you to follow the shark in a boat overnight, using a portable receiver.

This data shows the routes taken by two different sharks tracked between dusk and dawn. Both began near the top of the seamount and then swam into deeper water. The numbers on this contour map show the depth of the water.

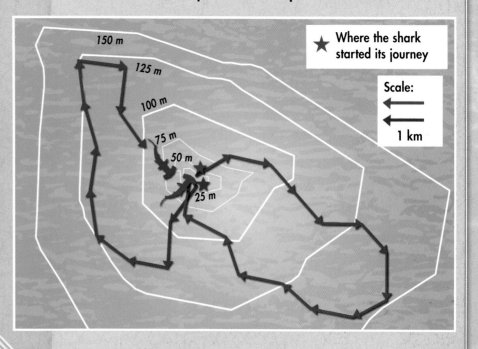

Q CHALLENGE QUESTIONS

1. How many kilometres did the red shark travel?
2. How many kilometres did the blue shark travel?
3. The sharks often made dives to the bottom. Which shark swam the deepest?
4. How deep did the blue shark dive?

KEEPING A SHARK IN CAPTIVITY

You've hurried back home for an event you wouldn't want to miss. A few weeks ago, a young great white shark was accidentally caught in a fishing net. You and your team rushed to help rescue her and care for her in an ocean pen. She's been doing well. Now she's ready to be moved to a huge tank at the aquarium. You've been looking forward to this day! You'll be able to study her closely while she lives at the aquarium.

FACTFILE

The young great white shark will live in this tank for perhaps a few months. If she does not do well, or when she gets too big, she will immediately be released back into the ocean.

- You helped to design this tank. When you did so, you had some important things to keep in mind.

- A great white shark would need plenty of room in a rounded tank. This tank holds nearly four million litres of water!

- Sharks are very sensitive to mild electric currents that might come from pumps or lightning. Electrical equipment must be placed so the currents can't travel into the tank.

Many people come to watch and admire the shark. You hope they are gaining a new respect for great white sharks in particular and all sharks in general.

WORKSTATION

The time has come to move the shark from the pen to the aquarium. You and your crew work quickly and carefully.

- First you net her and lift her onto a stretcher.
- You handle her gently so that you don't scare her.
- You keep her gills wet so she can breathe while she is on the stretcher.
- You transfer her to a specially designed 11,000-litre portable tank on wheels called a 'Tunabago'.
- You drive her to the aquarium and release her into her new home!

You watch as she explores her new surroundings. Your most important job now is making sure that she is eating well.

At her age, one year, she should be growing quickly. You've been keeping careful records of how much food she is eating. She should be eating 1.5% of her body weight every day. Once she starts eating that much, she will be ready to live in the new tank at the aquarium. She needs to continue to eat at least that much from now on.

You have weighed the shark every 25 days. Here are your notes for the first 200 days:

Day	1	25	50	75	100	125	150	175	200
Weight of shark (kg)	23	24	29	31	34	37	38	42	45
Weight of food eaten (kg)	0.18	0.36	0.44	0.53	0.54	0.59	0.84	0.63	0.68
Percentage of body weight	0.8%	1.5%	1.5%	1.7%	1.6%	1.6%	2.2%	1.5%	1.5%

CHALLENGE QUESTIONS

1. On which day did the shark begin eating well enough to be transferred to the aquarium?

2. When did she gain more than 4 kilograms in 25 days?

3. What was the first day that she ate more than 1.5% of her body weight?

4. During the period of time before Day 150, you tried giving her a different type of food. Do you think she liked it? How do you know?

As a shark biologist, you want to help people learn more about sharks. Many people only know that some sharks can be dangerous. They don't know how important they are. Other people don't understand that sharks are becoming endangered. About 100 million of them are killed every year for their fins. You do all you can to help people realise why sharks should be protected.

 FACTFILE

People often ask what they can do to stay safe when they go swimming. You have some good advice for them.

- Swim with a group of people and stay close to shore.

- Don't swim where there are seals or sea lions.

- Don't wear sparkly jewellery in the water. A shark may think it is the glint of a fish's scales.

- Don't swim at night, dawn or dusk.

- Watch for diving sea birds. They may be after small fish that could also attract sharks.

- Don't try to touch, or otherwise annoy, a shark!

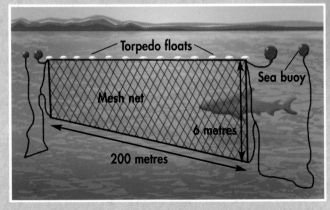

Torpedo floats

Sea buoy

Mesh net

6 metres

200 metres

On some beaches, nets like these are used to keep sharks from coming into contact with people. However, other marine life can get tangled up in these nets, and die.

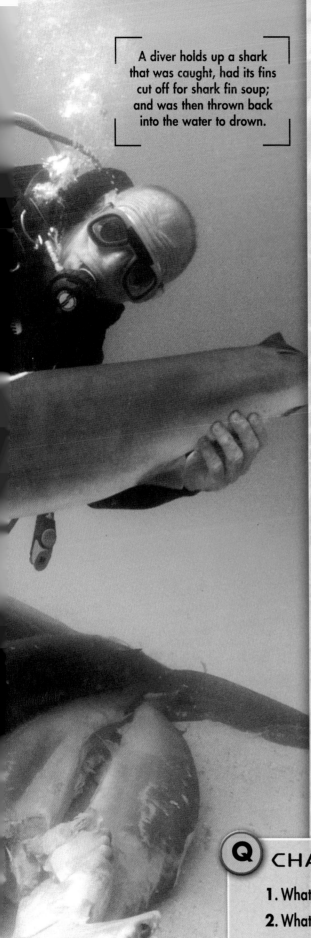

A diver holds up a shark that was caught, had its fins cut off for shark fin soup; and was then thrown back into the water to drown.

Why are sharks important?

- They help to control the size of the populations beneath them on the food chain. This keeps a balance of plant and animal life.
- They eat weak and unhealthy animals. This improves the health of the animals that are left. It also cuts down on competition among those animals for food and space.

Why have so many been killed?

- They are killed out of fear and for sport. They are also killed for body parts to sell as souvenirs (such as jaws and teeth); or for food.
- 270,000 sharks worldwide are killed every day, just for their flesh or fins.

Shark fin soup is a valued meal in some cultures.

If the population gets too low, can it recover?

- It is unlikely. We have been catching sharks faster than they can reproduce.
- Some fish can produce thousands of eggs at a time, but a great white shark female can only produce 12–14 pups per breeding season.

Q CHALLENGE QUESTIONS

1. What is one problem with using shark nets?
2. What two parts of the shark are eaten most often?
3. How do sharks help keep ocean populations in balance?
4. What two reasons explain why a shark population does not grow quickly?

TIPS FOR SCIENCE SUCCESS

Pages 6-7

Shark Biologist

The sharks in these pictures share certain similarities because they belong to one of the 34 shark families. Sharks don't all look alike. They often eat different things, live in different places, and behave in different ways.

Pages 8-9

The Design of a Shark

All sharks have shared characteristics. This includes the way their bodies are put together. If you compare a great white or a hammerhead shark to the huge whale shark or the tiny pygmy shark, you'll find they have many things in common. These similarities include skeleton, skin, and arrangement of fins (although some have a few more fins than others).

Pages 10-11

Shark Necropsy

This is much like the way doctors and crime investigators look inside a human body to find out what caused the person to die. Sometimes the smallest things can bring down a large organism. In this case, many tiny shrimp-like copepods weakened the shark and brought about its death.

Pages 12-13

Leaping Sharks!

Many animals show off in one way or another to get the attention of the opposite sex. Also, when organisms are hungry they will make an extra effort to catch the food that is most useful to them. A seal's high percentage of blubber will provide a shark with the most amount of energy.

Pages 14-15

Top Predators

Every living thing is part of a food chain. In fact, most are usually part of a few different food chains. These join up to make a food web. Most animals are in the middle of the chain, trying to eat while not becoming something else's dinner. Like sharks, we are at the top of our food chains.

Pages 16-17

Staying Warm in Cold Water

Sharks are one of the few types of fish that are warm-bodied rather than cold-blooded. When it's cold outside, cold-blooded animals such as reptiles and most fish have to warm up before they can move very well. That's why you often see a snake or lizard sunning itself on a rock.

Pages 20-21

Tagging Sharks

Satellite tagging has made it possible to find out things about animal behaviour that we couldn't have learned otherwise. In the past sharks were tagged with a simple plastic tag. Scientists couldn't find out where that shark went unless it was killed and someone sent them the tag. All scientists could tell was where the shark was when it was tagged, and where it ended up when it died. Now we can follow the movements of sharks as they go about their lives.

Pages 26-27

Keeping a Shark in Captivity

Some types of sharks adapt well to living in an aquarium. Many attempts have been made to keep a great white shark in captivity. None were successful for more than a few days. Then, in 2003, a young female great white shark was kept in a four million-litre tank at Monterey Bay Aquarium, USA. She was released after 198 days.

Pages 28-29

Looking to the Future

There are many different careers in the field of marine biology. Someone who wants to be a marine biologist or scientist should work hard at Maths and Science in school. It's also good to learn as much as possible about computers and technology.

Pages 6-7

1. Whale shark.
2. Spined pygmy shark.
3. Seven.
4. Fish, shellfish, squid.

Pages 8-9

1. A tooth in the next row replaces it.
2. Its skin is covered in sharp denticles.
3. Dorsal, pectoral, pelvic, anal, caudal.
4. Dorsal and pectoral.

Pages 10-11

1. Copepods in its gills.
2. The liver.
3. It had no cuts or bruises, which usually show a shark has died in a fight.
4. Swim forward, face into a current, move its gill covers, or pump water across its gills with its fins.

Pages 12-13

1. Twice: C and G.
2. Six times.
3. Feeding.
4. Prey was present in six of the eight observed jumps. Potential mates were present in only two of the observed jumps.

Pages 14-15

1. Hammerhead shark, squid, sardine.
2. Rays, tuna, squid and lobster.
3. Crabs, shrimp, sardines, young fish.
4. Their numbers might decrease quickly, because there would be many more squid to eat them.

Pages 16-17

1. Elephant seals, California sea lions, harbour seals, Northern fur seals.
2. They are all seals.
3. Seals have blubber.
4. Whales also have blubber; and sharks don't have to hunt them if they're dead!

Pages 18-19

1. Wolves and alligators.
2. Their shape is similar when seen from below.
3. Because when it tasted the camera, it found out that the camera wasn't food.

Pages 20-21

1. Acoustic.
2. Satellite.
3. Acoustic.
4. Satellite.

Pages 22-23

1. Summer: one week; winter: two weeks.
2. Autumn.
3. No.
4. No.

Pages 24-25

1. 14 kilometres.
2. 12 kilometres.
3. The red shark.
4. 150 metres.

Pages 26-27

1. Day 25.
2. Days 50 and 175.
3. Day 75.
4. Yes. She ate more food than usual.

Pages 28-29

1. Other animals get trapped in them and die.
2. Fins and flesh.
3. They control the populations below them on the food chains.
4. They don't have many babies in their lifetime; and they may get killed faster than they can reproduce.

For more information about shark conservation, please visit these websites:

www.bite-back.com

www.montereybayaquarium.org

AUTOPSY A careful, detailed examination of a person's body and organs after death, usually to try to find out what caused the person's death.

CARNIVORE An animal that eats mainly meat.

CARTILAGE A strong, flexible tissue that in certain animals forms all or part of the skeleton, rather than bone.

CONSERVE To work toward saving and protecting natural resources.

CONSUMER An animal that get the food it needs by eating other animals or plants.

COPEPODS Very small ocean-dwelling shrimp-like creatures that usually measure less than 4mm long. Thousands of copepods, sometimes more than one kind, can live on a single shark.

DIVERSITY A variety of different species.

FOOD CHAIN An arrangement of organisms in an ecosystem that shows who eats what.

FREE-DIVING Diving underwater without the help of diving equipment. Free-divers hold their breath underwater.

HERBIVORE An animal that only eats plants.

HYDRODYNAMIC SHAPE A streamlined shape that allows a shark or fish to move easily through the water.

HYPOTHESIS An educated guess as to how or why something happens.

INTERCONTINENTAL Between different continents.

MIGRATION Seasonal movement from one place to another.

NECROPSY An autopsy performed on an animal.

OMNIVORE An animal that eats both plants and animals.

PREDATOR An animal that kills and eats other animals for food.

PREDICTABLE When it is possible to estimate that something will happen.

PREY An animal that is eaten by other animals.

PRODUCER A green plant that makes its own food using energy from the Sun.

PUP The young of some mammals, and sharks.

SCUBA DIVING Swimming underwater using self-contained breathing equipment.

SEAMOUNT A mountain rising from the ocean floor that is not high enough to break the surface of the water.

SPECIES Organisms that are similar in structure and are able to reproduce among themselves.

WARM-BODIED The ability of some animals to keep parts of their body warmer than the surrounding water or air.

PICTURE CREDITS
(l=left, r=right, t=top, c=centre, b=bottom)
Alamy: 1 (main) Visual & Written SL, 2t Stephen Frink Collection, 6-7 (main) Stephen Frink Collection, 7tl JUPITERIMAGES/Comstock Images, 7tr David Fleetham, 7cl Donald Nausbaum, 7cc Jeff Rotman, 7br, 19t David Fleetham. Ardea & Getty composite: 14-15 (main). Corbis: 28-29 (main) Jeffrey L. Rotman. David Scharf/Science Faction 11b. Getty: 7cr, 8-9 (main) Norbert Wu. Mike Parry/Minden Pictures/FLPA: ofc. NHPA: 17 row 4/c TAKETOMO SHIRATORI. naturepl.com: 7tc, 10-11 (main) Jeff Rotman, 12-13 (main) Andrew Parkinson, 12bl, 16-17 (main) Tony Heald, 20-21 (main) Jurgen Freund, 22-23 (main) Doug Perrine, 29b Doug Perrine, 31r Doug Perrine, 30-31 (main), 32 (main) Doug Perrine. Oxford Scientific: 9b Roger De La Harpe/Africa Imagery, 11c Phototake Inc, 17 row 4/l Chris and Monique Fallows/Apex Images, 17 row 5/r, 24-25(main) Gerard Soury. Reuters: 7bl. Rex Features: 18-19 (main). Science Photo Library: 9t, 17 row 2/l, 26-27 (main). Shutterstock: obc tl, obc br, 9c Kristian Sekulic, 7bc Ian Scott, 8b Byelolutska Mariya, 12b Ian Scott, 17 row 1/l Rebecca Dickerson, 17 row 1/c MaxFX, 17 row 1/r David Hughes, 17 row 2/c Steve Schwettman, 17 row 2/r Bill Kennedy, 17 row 3/l Ariel Bravy, 17 row 3/c Michael Ransburg, 17 row 3/r Kristian Sekulic, 17 row 4/r Wolfgang Amri, 17 row 5/l Brent Reeves, 17 row 5/c J. Helgason, 24b Ian Scott, 29t Karen Winton, 30l Ian Scott, 30tr Kristian Sekulic, 30cr Ian Scott. ticktock media archive: 10b, 12c, 15t, 19c, 21c, 22c, 23t, 25c, 28b.
Every effort has been made to trace the copyright holders, and we apologise in advance for any unintentional omissions. We would be pleased to insert the appropriate acknowledgments in any subsequent edition of this publication.